20 Parables of Jesus
20 Short Stories for Kids

Written by Nina Gill
Illustrations by Chanel Christy

HEAD LION

The Workers in the Vineyard

Once, there was a landowner who had a vineyard. Early in the morning, he hired some workers and agreed on a fair wage. Later, he hired more workers throughout the day, promising to pay what's right. At the end of the day, everyone got the same pay, no matter when they started.

The Lesson

The story teaches that God's love and rewards are for everyone, no matter when we start following Him.

The Parable of the Workers in the Vineyard is found in the Bible in the Gospel of Matthew, chapter 20, verses 1-16.

The Pearl of Great Price

A rich merchant collected treasures and expensive pearls. One day, he found the most exquisite pearl ever seen. Its beauty captivated him. Determined, he sold all he had to buy it.

The Lesson

The kingdom of heaven is worth more than anything, and giving up everything for it is the best choice.

The Parable of the Pearl of Great Price is found in the Bible in the Gospel of Matthew, chapter 13, verse 46.

The Lost Sheep

A shepherd had 100 sheep, but one little sheep goes missing. The shepherd, who loves all his sheep, leaves the 99 and goes searching until he finds the lost one. When he does, he's so happy and throws a big party.

The Lesson

It's all about how much God cares for each of us and celebrates when even one person turns back to Him. Just like the shepherd, God never gives up on us and loves us so much!t

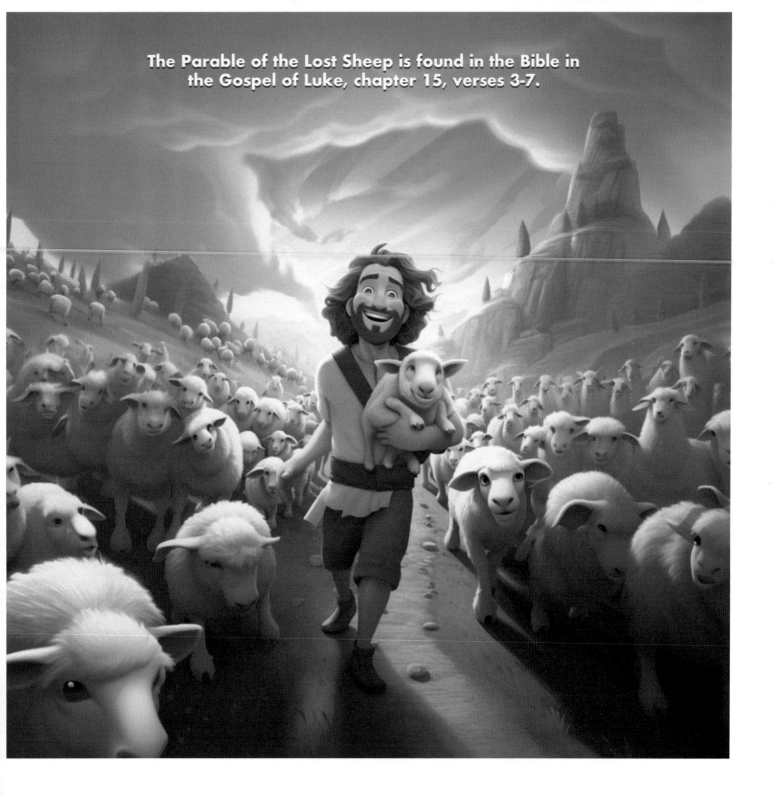

The Parable of the Lost Sheep is found in the Bible in the Gospel of Luke, chapter 15, verses 3-7.

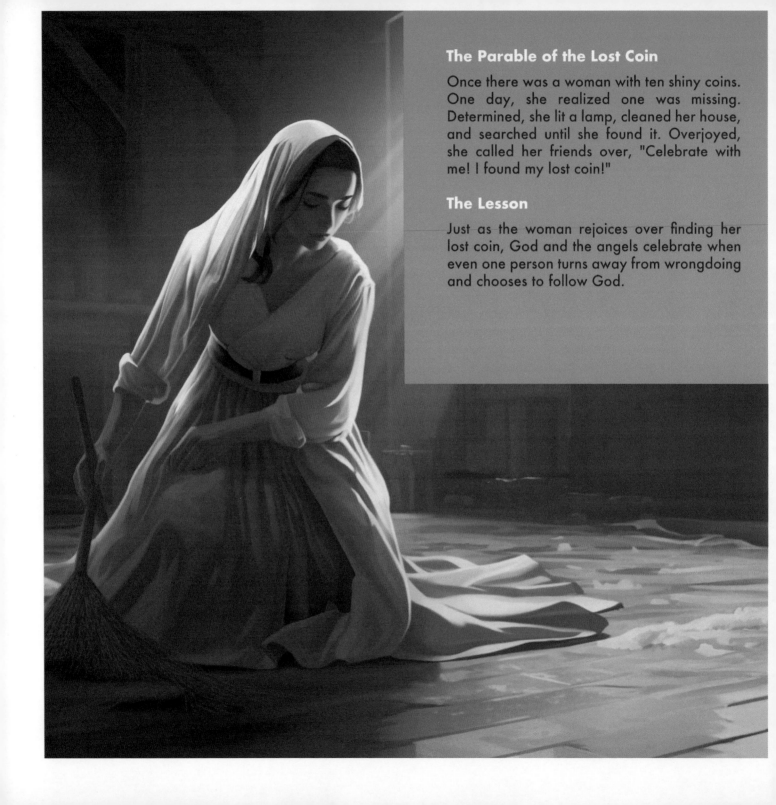

The Parable of the Lost Coin

Once there was a woman with ten shiny coins. One day, she realized one was missing. Determined, she lit a lamp, cleaned her house, and searched until she found it. Overjoyed, she called her friends over, "Celebrate with me! I found my lost coin!"

The Lesson

Just as the woman rejoices over finding her lost coin, God and the angels celebrate when even one person turns away from wrongdoing and chooses to follow God.

The Parable of the Lost Coin is found in the Bible in the Gospel of Luke, chapter 15, verses 8-10.

The Parable of the Rich Man and Lazarus

A rich man lived in luxury, ignoring a poor, sick man named Lazarus outside his gate. Both died, and Lazarus went to a good place, while the rich man faced suffering. He asked for help but couldn't get it.

The Lesson

The story teaches us to care for others, listen to God, and not wait until it's too late.

The Parable of the Rich Man and Lazarus is found in the Bible in the Gospel of Luke, chapter 16, verses 19-31.

The Parable of the Pharisee and the Tax Collector

Once, a Pharisee and a Tax Collector went to the temple. The Pharisee loudly thanked God for how good he was. The tax collector, who felt sorry for his mistakes, cried, asked for forgiveness.

The Lesson

The story teaches us that saying sorry and being humble is more important to God than showing off.

The Parable of the Pharisee and the Tax Collector is found in the Bible in the Gospel of Luke, chapter 18, verses 9-14.

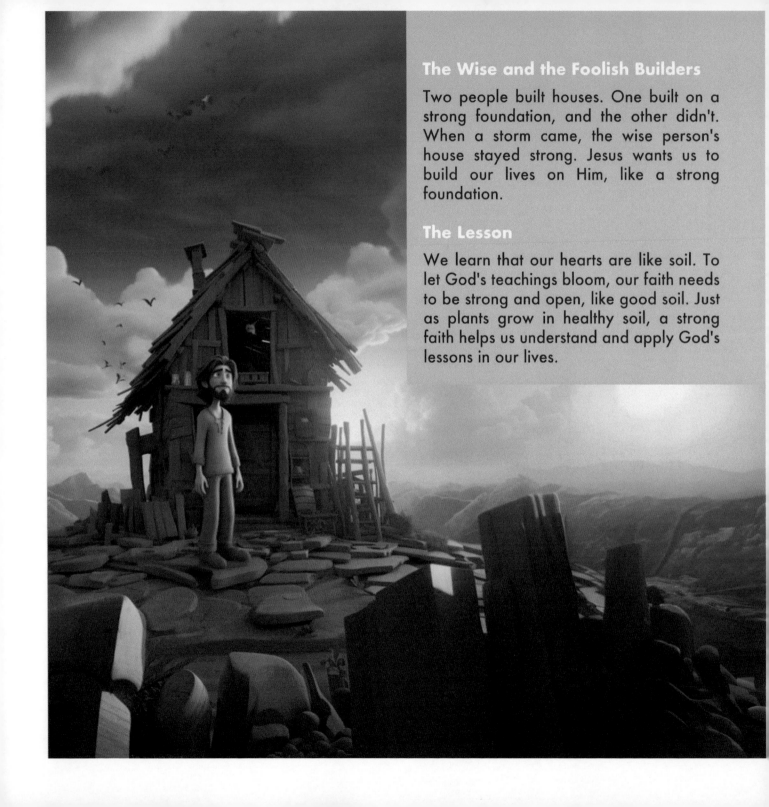

The Wise and the Foolish Builders

Two people built houses. One built on a strong foundation, and the other didn't. When a storm came, the wise person's house stayed strong. Jesus wants us to build our lives on Him, like a strong foundation.

The Lesson

We learn that our hearts are like soil. To let God's teachings bloom, our faith needs to be strong and open, like good soil. Just as plants grow in healthy soil, a strong faith helps us understand and apply God's lessons in our lives.

The Parable of the Wise and Foolish Builders is found in the Bible in the Gospel of Matthew, chapter 7, verses 24-27.

The Mustard Seed

The Mustard Seed parable teaches that small things can have big impacts. Like a tiny seed growing into a large tree, our faith and good deeds can grow immensely.

The Lesson

Small acts of kindness and faith can grow into something big and wonderful. Just like a tiny seed turns into a giant tree, our small efforts can make a huge, positive impact in the world!

The Parable of the Mustard Seed can be found in the Bible in the Gospel of Matthew, chapter 13, verse 31-32, and also in the Gospel of Luke, chapter 13, verse 18-19.

The Parable of the Great Banquet

A man planned a big dinner and invited many friends. When it was time, he sent his servant to tell them to come. But everyone had excuses – one bought a field, another got oxen, and someone just got married. The man was sad, so he invited others who were happy to come.

The Lesson

God's love is for everyone, no matter who they are. In the story, some people made excuses and couldn't come to the party. But, God invites everyone, and it doesn't matter if they are rich or poor, or what they have done. Those who believe in God and accept His invitation are always welcome.

The Parable of the Great Banquet is found in the Bible in the Gospel of Luke, chapter 14, verses 16-24.

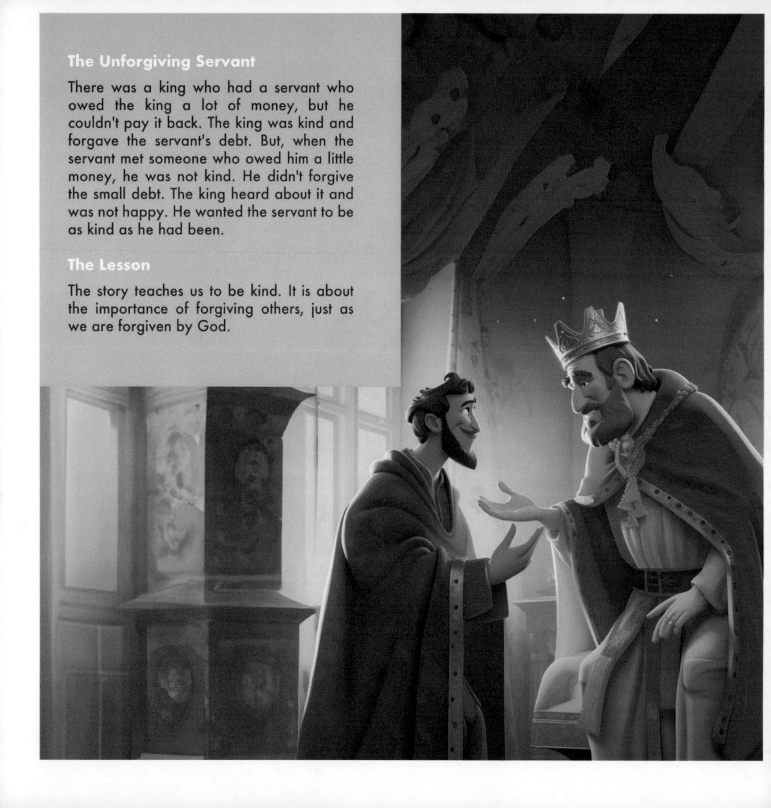

The Unforgiving Servant

There was a king who had a servant who owed the king a lot of money, but he couldn't pay it back. The king was kind and forgave the servant's debt. But, when the servant met someone who owed him a little money, he was not kind. He didn't forgive the small debt. The king heard about it and was not happy. He wanted the servant to be as kind as he had been.

The Lesson

The story teaches us to be kind. It is about the importance of forgiving others, just as we are forgiven by God.

The Parable of the Unforgiving Servant is found in the Bible in the Gospel of Matthew, chapter 18, verses 21-35.

The Good Shepherd

Once upon a time, there was a good shepherd who loved his sheep very much. He would do anything to keep them safe, even if it meant facing danger himself. Unlike a hired worker, the good shepherd stayed with the sheep, protecting them from wolves. He was a true friend to the sheep, always looking out for their well-being.

The Lesson

Jesus is like a super caring shepherd who loves his sheep so much. He would even protect them from scary wolves, even if it means he might get hurt. But there are some, when trouble comes, they might run away. Jesus stays and keeps us safe because he really, really cares about us.

The Parable of the Good Shepherd is found in the Bible in the Gospel of John, chapter 10, verses 11-18.

The Parable of the Persistent Widow

Once, there was a judge who didn't care about God or people. In the same town, a persistent widow asked him for justice against her enemy. The judge ignored her for a while, but because she kept asking, he finally gave in.

The Lesson

The story teaches us that we can keep talking to God, and He will answer our prayers because He loves us.

The Parable of the Persistent Widow is found in the Bible in the Gospel of Luke, chapter 18, verses 1-8.

The Prodigal Son

A father had two sons. One son asked for his share of the money and left. He spent everything but realized he made a mistake. When he came home, his father was overjoyed and forgave him.

'Prodigal' means someone who wastes their money and time.

The Lesson

The story shows that God loves us no matter what. If we make mistakes but say sorry and want to do better, God forgives us. It's like a big, warm hug from God. The lesson is that God's love is unconditional; we just need to ask for forgiveness and try to be our best selves.

The Parable of the Prodigal Son is found in the Bible in the Gospel of Luke, chapter 15, verses 11-32.

The Rich Fool

Once, a man had so many crops that he didn't know where to store them. Instead of sharing with others, he decided to build even bigger barns for himself. He thought he could relax and enjoy life. But God said, "You're foolish! Tonight, your life will end. What will happen to all you stored for yourself?"

The Lesson

The story teaches that life is about more than just having lots of stuff. It's about caring for people and being generous. Also, it reminds us that life is short, and any day we can meet God, so it's important to focus on what really matters in our hearts and be prepared.

The parable of the rich man is found in the Bible in the
Gospel of Luke, chapter 12, verses 16-20.

The Good Samaritan

Once upon a time, a man got hurt, and many people walked past him without helping. But then, a kind Samaritan, who wasn't usually friends with the injured man, stopped. The Samaritan showed that being kind to others is really important by taking care of the hurt man and making sure he got the help he needed.

The Lesson

The Good Samaritan story teaches us to be kind to everyone, even if they're different. Just like the Samaritan helped a hurt man, we should help our friends, neighbors, and even strangers. It's about treating everyone with kindness and showing love to those who need it.

The Parable of the Good Samaritan is found in the Bible in the Gospel of Luke, chapter 10, verses 25-37

The Sower and the Seeds

Once, a farmer went out to plant seeds in his field. Some seeds fell on the path, some on rocky ground, some among thorns, and some on good soil. The ones on the path got eaten by birds, the rocky ground seeds couldn't grow deep roots, and the thorns choked others. But the seeds in good soil grew into strong, healthy plants.

The Lesson

When we listen to God's words and follow them, our hearts become like good soil, ready to grow and learn

The Parable of the Sower and the Seeds is found in the Bible in the Gospel of Matthew, chapter 13, verses 1-23, and also in the Gospels of Mark (Mark 4:1-20) and Luke (Luke 8:4-15).

The Three Servants and the Talents

Once, a master gave money to his three servants before going away. Five bags for one, two for another, and one for the last. The first two invested and doubled their money, making the master happy. But the third buried his money and didn't make more. When the master returned, he praised the first two but was disappointed in the third for not using the money wisely.

The Lesson

God gives everyone time, skills, and special gifts. We're like caretakers, using these gifts well makes them grow. We're accountable to God for how we use His gifts.

The Parable of the Talents is found in the Bible in the Gospel of Matthew, chapter 25, verses 14-30.

The Parable of the Vine and Branches

Once, Jesus told a special story about a vine and its branches. He said, "I am the vine, and you are the branches. If you stay connected to me, you'll grow and be fruitful. But if you don't, it's like a branch without the vine—it won't bear fruit."

The Lesson

Always stay close to Jesus, and you'll do amazing things together.

The parable of the Vine and the Branches is found in the Bible in the Gospel of John, chapter 15, verses 1-17.

The Parable of the Ten Virgins

Once, ten excited friends were waiting for a wedding to start. Five of them were very clever and brought extra lamp oil, but the other five didn't. When the bridegroom finally arrived, it was dark, and the wise friends had enough light. The others had to go get more oil and missed the fun celebration.

The Lesson

Always be ready for when Jesus comes back. Be kind, loving, and do good things every day. That way, when Jesus returns, it's like being all set for the best celebration ever.

The Parable of the Ten Virgins is found in the Bible in the Gospel of Matthew, chapter 25, verses 1-13.

The Wedding Feast

Once, a kind King threw a huge dinner for his son's wedding. He invited many guests, but some didn't want to come. The King told his servants to invite everyone they could find. People from everywhere joined the celebration. However, there was one person not dressed properly, just there for the fun. The King asked him to leave, enjoying the feast with those truly happy for his son.

The Lesson

The story shows God's love is like an invitation for everyone, but we must also prepare for judgment day, not just seek rewards.

The Parable of the Wedding Feast is found in the Bible in the Gospel of Matthew, chapter 22, verses 1-14.

To the children all around the world,
may you find comfort in the embrace of faith, like a cozy blanket that wraps around you.

Published 2023
Print ISBN: 979-8-9895130-6-2
Ebook ISBN: 979-8-9895130-7-9

For information or speaker assignments you can send an email
You can also connect with Nina on Facebook, Instagram, & Linkedin

About Nina Gill

Nina Gill is dedicated to the emotional well-being and education of children. A successful family physician in her native country, she embraced the role of an educator when she moved to North America. Today, her passion lies in special education along with mental health, where she helps parents and children navigate behavioral challenges, especially those teetering on the edge of autism, ADHD, or learning disabilities.

With a Master's in Instructional Science, an Executive MBA, and a Bachelor's in Medicine, Nina blends her medical knowledge with a knack for teaching. Her students thrive under her guidance, boasting a perfect pass rate that speaks to her unwavering dedication.

Embracing the power of faith, Nina strives to create a nurturing and inspiring environment for every young mind to flourish. With a staunch Christian belief, she passionately advocates for faith-based teaching to enrich education today.

Printed in Great Britain
by Amazon

58244446R00025